D1070459

Greenhaven World History Program

GENERAL EDITORS

Malcolm Yapp
Margaret Killingray
Edmund O'Connor

Cover design by John Castle

ISBN 0-89908-005-7 Paper Edition
ISBN 0-89908-030-8 Library Edition

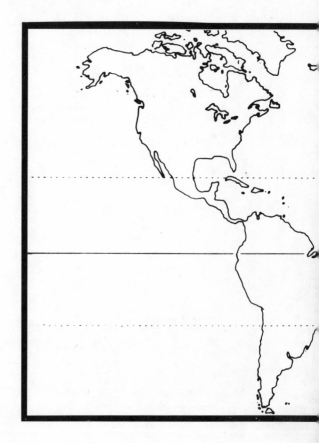

First published in Great Britain 1974 by
GEORGE G. HARRAP & CO. LTD
© George G. Harrap & Co. Ltd 1974

CHINGIS KHAN
AND THE MONGOL EMPIRE

by Malcolm Yapp

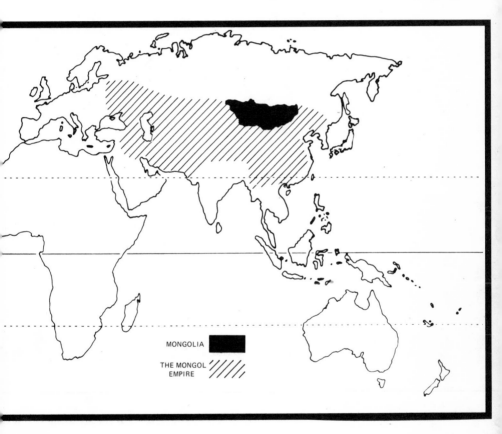

MONGOLIA

THE MONGOL
EMPIRE

Greenhaven Press, Inc.
577 SHOREVIEW PARK ROAD
ST. PAUL, MN 55112

Mongolian Terrain

In 1238 Matthew Paris, a monk in the great abbey of St Albans in England, wrote that herrings were very cheap. This was because the merchants who came every year from the Baltic countries to buy herrings had not arrived that year. Their own countries had been disturbed by the attacks of a strange people they called Tatars.

In this way the effects of happenings thirty years earlier in remote Mongolia reached distant England. What had happened in Mongolia was the uniting of the Mongol people by a man named Temujin, better known as Chingis Khan.

THE MONGOLS

Mongolia is a high flat land much of which is desert. In winter it is bitterly cold: in summer fiercely hot. The fearsome Gobi desert covers a large part of the south. In the north there are mountains, hills, streams, and forests and life is possible there. Even now, life is very different from life elsewhere; in the thirteenth century it was totally different from the life Matthew Paris knew in England.

Very few Mongols lived in houses and farmed the soil. Some lived in forests and hunted. Most lived in tents made of felt, kept sheep, goats and horses, and roamed the great plains in search of good grass for their animals. They were what we call *nomads.* (D1-4) *

The Mongols were hard, tough men. They had flat faces and thick yellowy skins. They ate meat, cheese and *curds* (soured milk). Their favourite drink was fermented mare's milk which they called *kumiss.* (D5-7) They liked to get drunk on this. Because their

*The reference (D) indicates the numbered documents at the end of this book.

A Mongol Camp

life was so hard, settled people looked down on them and said they were backward. The Mongols did not think so. They were proud of their way of life. They thought it was the best and freest way to live. They looked down on farmers whom they regarded as little better than slaves.

Most often the Mongols moved about in small family groups — a man, his wives, brothers, children and grandchildren. Sometimes one of these 'extended' families would join with other families, especially for hunting. Then the Mongols would ride for many miles, making a great noise, driving wild animals before them until they reached a central meeting place. There the animals were penned and slaughtered to provide meat for months ahead.

Some of the Mongols were Christians, and some Buddhists; others knew of Islam, but most of them had their own religion and customs. There were many gods; living in woods, rivers, stones, animals and mountains. The greatest god, Tengri, lived in the sky. His name — the Eternal Blue Heaven — tells us something about the climate of Mongolia. The Mongols were superstitious. They had witch-doctors or

A Mongol Tent

shamans (hence the name of the religion, shamanism), who told stories and performed magical tricks.

The Mongols had some contacts with the people around them. They needed grain, metal goods and other products from the settled peoples. Chinese traders and Muslims from Turkestan brought such goods to the *steppes,* as the great plains of Asia are called, and exchanged them for animals and furs. Occasionally the Mongols raided other people in search of loot. It was to keep out such raids that the Chinese had built the Great Wall many years before. But these raids were no real danger to China. Only a few Mongols took part. Mostly the Mongols fought among themselves. The Chinese encouraged this because it made the Mongols less of a nuisance to them.

The Mongols had no political unity. Each family looked after

A Mongol Woman at her Tent Door

Medieval Tatar Huts and Wagons

its own affairs. Sometimes a chief would attract followers because of his skill in battle or hunting. Sometimes poor families would join more powerful groups for protection. But no-one ruled all Mongolia. Instead there were several *confederations* (loosely organized groups), each with its own chief. In the year 1200 the Mongols were just one such confederation. They lived in the north-east around the headwaters of the Onon and Kerulen rivers. Other confederations were more powerful and prosperous, such as the Keraits of central Mongolia or the Turkish Naymans of the west. Some were more savage like the hated Tatars of the east and the forest-dwelling Merkits and Oyrats of the far north.

CHINGIS KHAN

Temujin was born in 1167. His father, who was a notable chief from an old royal family, died, possibly poisoned by Tatars, when Temujin was only nine. His family then became very poor, lost most of their flocks and Temujin and his brothers had to live by hunting. It was a hard life, but Temujin was harder. When his half-brother annoyed him he killed him. Once he was taken prisoner by a rival tribe, but escaped.

Gradually there came better times. Temujin got more animals. He also married. His wife, Borte, was a wise woman and as tough as her husband. They had not been married long when she was captured by Merkit raiders. Temujin fled, deciding to save himself and

Mongol Horseman with Killed Game

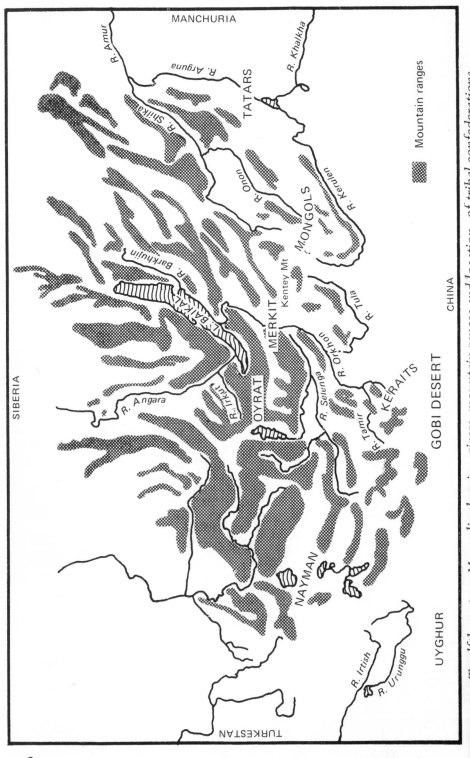

his horses. Many months later he rescued her with the help of a more powerful chief, Toghril, of the Kerait confederation. Temujin was still only a minor chief and needed a protector. But after this he began to show his own skill and attracted his own loyal followers. By 1196 he was ready to make his own bid for power in Mongolia.

We do not know very much about the years 1196-1206 when Temujin, now known by his title of Chingis Khan, became supreme. *The Secret History of the Mongols* tells only Chingis's side of the story. In it his actions are always good and his enemies are bad. But good and bad meant very different things to the Mongols than they do to us. So, reading the *Secret History* is like looking into a strange world in which what we would think to be small things have great importance and the things we think important are not even mentioned.

But we can follow the ups and downs of Chingis's career. There are battles and massacres, continual betrayals and a long

Chingis Khan

rivalry with a friend of his youth named Januka. One after another Chingis killed his rivals, in battle or by deceit. One was a royal prince named Buri, who was a great wrestler. Chingis arranged a 'friendly' match with one of his own brothers who broke Buri's neck. Eventually Chingis

Mongol Soldiers with Pack Horses and Camels

Mongol Archers

Mongol Warrior

THE MONGOL ARMY

But first he had to organize his army. (D10) Every Mongol man was liable for service. Family heads brought their warriors to the tribal chiefs who in turn brought their troops to the great generals under Chingis himself. A special corps of chosen warriors formed Chingis's own personal guard. Like the Roman army, the Mongol army was organized on a decimal system. But, unlike the Roman army, it was almost entirely cavalry.

The Mongols were the greatest horsemen in the world; standing in their big wooden stirrups on their small tireless horses they could ride for days.

Their armour was leather with steel caps. Their favourite weapon was the bow. In battle they moved in quickly, fired their arrows and slipped out again, only to turn and swoop upon another part of the enemy force. Their speed helped to make the enemy think that their numbers were much greater than they were.

The military skill of the Mongols was the secret of their victories. They were hard, ruthless and could fight on horseback better than anyone else. Until guns were invented light cavalry were unbeatable in open battle.

triumphed. First he massacred the Tatars to win east Mongolia. (D8) Next was the turn of the Keraits and central Mongolia. In 1204 he hunted down the Merkits of the north. Those who were not killed were attached to Mongol tribes. All therefore became Mongols. To celebrate his final victory he held a great council in 1206. He was now proclaimed Great Khan by all and he raised his new standard. (D9) This white standard with nine horsetails was to become feared throughout the world.

THE CAMPAIGNS OF CHINGIS

China was the first and greatest prize. At the time of Chingis it was

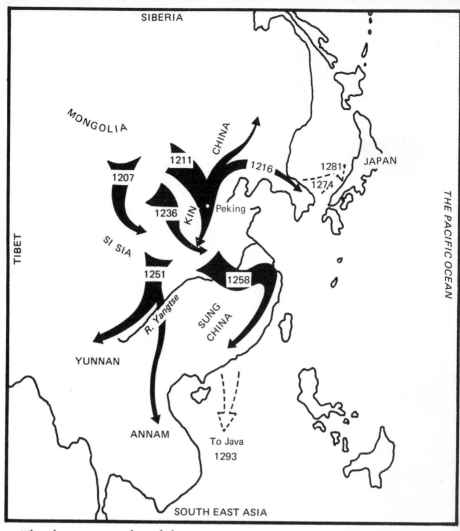

The three main political divisions existing c. 1200 in China (Arrows with dates show the direction of Mongol campaigns)

divided into three parts. South of the Yangtse river which flows from from west to east through the heart of China was the Sung empire. That was still safe for many years from the Mongols. It was finally defeated by Chingis's grandson Khublay Khan in 1279. North of the Yangtse were two states. In the west was the small state of Si-Sia. Chingis defeated this by 1209. In the east was the Kin empire with its capital at Peking. The Mongols attacked the Kins in 1211. The Kins took longer to defeat because, although unbeatable in the open, the Mongols had not yet learned how to attack forts and walled towns. But, by destroying the crops, they eventually starved the towns into surrender. In 1215 Peking was looted and burned.

The campaigns in China continued. For the Mongols China was always the most important country after Mongolia. But Chingis could now turn his attention to the west.

To the west of Mongolia is Turkestan. The Turks were people very similar to the Mongols in their way of life. They too were nomads. Some, especially those in eastern Turkestan, had remained nomads. Among these were the Uyghurs. These people lived south of the Tien Shan mountains. They had become Buddhists and Christians and had learned to write down their language. Chingis absorbed them peacefully into his empire. This was very important for the development of the Mongols. As fellow nomads they could understand and respect each other. The Mongols were much more ready to learn from the Uyghurs than from settled peoples. So the Mongols learned to write their own language in Uyghur script and the Uyghurs became clerks in the government of the Mongols. In short, they helped to civilize the Mongols.

In the northern part of eastern Turkestan lived the Black Khitays. After Chingis had defeated the Naymans, a Nayman prince named Kuchluh had fled to the Black Khitays' land, and made himself king. Chingis sent his general Jebe to destroy Kuchluk. This he did and the way was open to western Turkestan.

For many years the Turks had been moving westwards. Some had remained nomads, moving along the great grasslands of southern Siberia into the Ukraine or passing south of the Caspian into Azerbaijan or even modern Turkey. Others, however, had abandoned the nomadic life and become soldiers and rulers in the lands of Islam. One such Turkish soldier was Sultan Muhammad, who ruled over western Turkestan. His capital was at Khwarazm or Khiva in the delta of the river Oxus, near where it flows into the Aral Sea.

Sultan Muhammad knew little of the Mongols. He thought he was the greatest ruler in the world. When Chingis sent a caravan of merchants and some ambassadors he allowed the caravan to be looted and killed one of the ambassadors.

This was enough for Chingis. He assembled his main army of between 100,000 and 150,000 men and attacked Turkestan in 1219. Great cities like Bukhara and Balkh were destroyed. Dams and irrigation works were destroyed and crops ruined. Workers were enslaved and sent to Mongolia to work. Sultan Muhammad fled westwards, but he was pursued. The cities of eastern Iran were looted. One Mongol party led by the generals Jebe and Subotei chased the Sultan until he died on an island in the Caspian. Then they continued through the Caucasus into the Ukraine where they defeated a Russian force before they turned east again. Chingis himself pursued the Sultan's son through Afghanistan into India. Not until 1223–25 did the Mongols make their slow way back to Mongolia, laden with spoils. (D11-13)

That was the last great campaign of Chingis. In 1227 he died fighting the rebellious people of Si-Sia. His last act was to order yet another massacre. His body

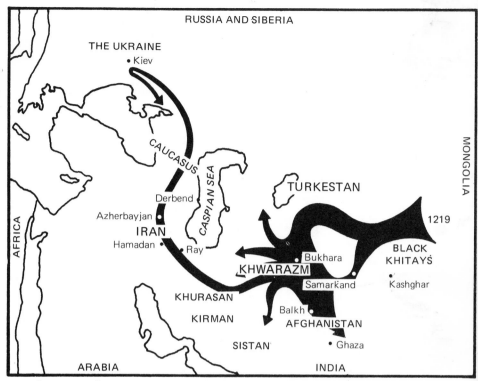

The Mongol campaigns of 1219-23 into the Middle East

was taken back to near his birthplace and buried secretly on the slopes of the sacred mountain of Kentey. The exact place is unknown.

To most people Chingis is one of the very bad men of history; but not to the Mongols. To them he was everything a man should be — brave, wise, just and honest. Even today he is the great national hero of Mongolia. He had given the Mongols unity, founded one of the great empires of the world, built up the army and the administration, laid down a strict code of laws (the Yasa), and begun the great victories in China and the west which his sons and grandsons were to complete.

THE MONGOL CONQUESTS

Chingis had four sons. To each he gave many Mongol and Turkish clans, their pasture lands and their taxes. The eldest, Juchi, received the western areas. The second and third sons, Chagatai and Ogetei, shared eastern Turkestan and western Mongolia. The youngest, Tuli, took most of Mongolia itself, while some of Chingis's brothers received shares in the east. Ogetei was also made Great Khan and ruled until 1241. He was followed by his son Guyuk. After Guyuk's death in 1248 there were quarrels among the other grandsons of Chingis. Guyuk's children were displaced by Mongke, the son of

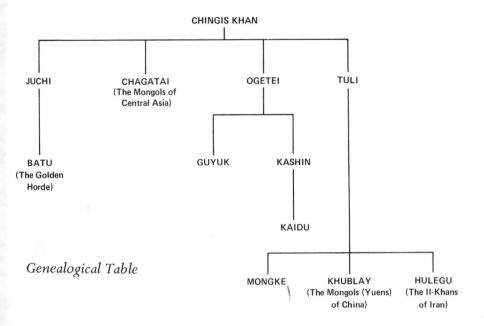

CHINGIS KHAN

JUCHI — CHAGATAI (The Mongols of Central Asia) — OGETEI — TULI

BATU (The Golden Horde)

GUYUK — KASHIN

KAIDU

Genealogical Table

MONGKE — KHUBLAY (The Mongols (Yuens) of China) — HULEGU (The Il-Khans of Iran)

Tuli. Mongke was supported by the sons of Juchi. Mongke ruled until 1259 and was succeeded by his brother the famous Khublay Khan. But in the reign of Khublay the Mongols became still more divided.

All this time the Mongol conquest continued. In 1236-42 a great horde of Mongols and Turks led by Batu, son of Juchi, invaded the Ukraine. Batu ravaged Russia, Poland and Hungary and his raids came near to Vienna. (D15-16) It was his Tatars of whom Matthew Paris wrote. But Batu did not return to Mongolia. He settled among the great pasture lands of the Ukraine and absorbed the Turkish nomads into what came to be called the Golden Horde. The Horde ruled the Russian states of the north for two hundred years and its successors terrorized them for much longer. (D17) Not until 1783 did the Russians annex the Crimea, the last remaining Tatar state.

In 1255—58 the west was again

Ogetai Khan

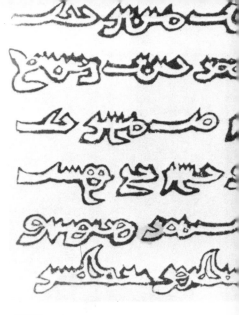

the target. This time it was the areas to the south of the Caspian Sea. These areas of the Middle East were the great centres of Muslim civilization, especially Baghdad, the city of the Caliphs, the successors of the Prophet Muhammad. The Mongols, led by Hulegu, brother of Mongke, conquered Iran, captured Baghdad, murdered the Caliph and so ended the Caliphate which had existed for six hundred years. The Mongols passed on into Syria before they were checked by the rulers of Egypt at the famous battle of Ayn Jalut in 1260. Then they turned back to Iran and Iraq to set up the Mongol state of the Il-Khans, which lasted for one hundred years.

Lastly, the Mongols completed the conquest of China. The Kins were defeated by 1235. Later the Mongols crossed the Yangtse and began the long struggle which ended in the defeat of the Sungs. A storm which destroyed the Mongol ships saved Japan from conquest but the Mongol armies fought their way into the jungles of south-east Asia, where many rulers recognized their authority.

At its greatest extent in the last years of the thirteenth century the Mongol empire stretched from the Pacific to the Mediterranean and from the China Sea to the Baltic. Except for the British Empire it was probably the largest empire the world has ever seen. What sort of empire was it?

Khublay Khan

THE MONGOL EMPIRE

The Mongol Empire was a nomad empire. Of course there have been many other nomad empires, like that of Attila the Hun, the Fulani of northern Nigeria and the Sioux of North America. But the Mongol Empire was easily the largest.

For nomads, land does not have

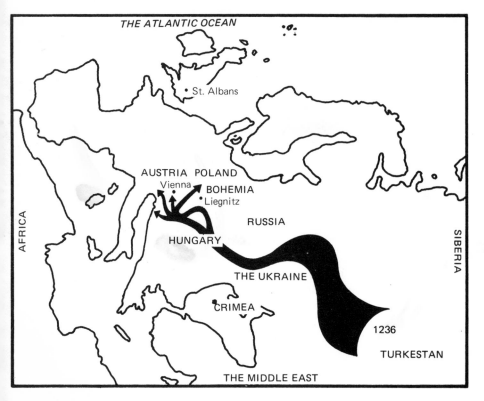

*The Mongol campaigns of 1236-42
into Russia and Central Europe*

The Mongol campaigns of 1255-58

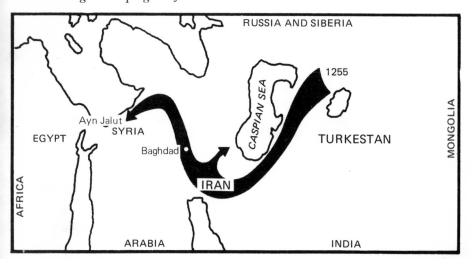

much significance. Men and animals matter most. Pastures are important but <u>true wealth is measured in sheep and horses. Settled people see things differently. For them land is important. That is where their food comes from and where their shelter is.</u> Unlike the nomads they cannot take their real wealth with them. So when the Mongols conquered land and settled they had to re-adjust their ideas of wealth and forms of government.

At first it seemed as if the nomadic way of life might become the principal way. The Mongols destroyed crops, dams, villages and towns. Large parts of the world might have become pasture land, just as actually happened in much of Turkestan. But the Mongols decided differently. They took advisers from China and from the muslim world who persuaded them that it was better to take regular taxes from the settled people than to destroy them. So the Mongols came to tolerate the settled peoples.

But toleration had dangers. At first the Mongol rulers ruled from Mongolia. A great new capital was built at Karakorum, to which came a stream of captured workers, princes, kings and ambassadors from as far as Europe. Later, however, the Mongol princes stopped sending their booty to Karakorum and began to live like kings themselves. So the Golden Horde in the west, the Il-Khans, and the Yuens of China became like separate states. In the middle grew up a new great nomad state under Kaidu, a descendant of Ogetei. Kaidu wanted the old Mongol ways, but the others were gradually changing as they found that the old religion and laws did not fit in their new states. The Il-Khans and the Golden Horde became Muslims; the Yuens took an interest in Buddhism and Confucianism. Gradually the princes drifted apart and fought each other. Then the settled peoples had their chance to recover. Finally the Mongols were either driven out or absorbed by the local population.

The Mongol empire fell for many reasons. One was the loss of unity. Another was that the empire was too big, both in numbers of people and in area. The whole population of Mongolia in the thirteenth century was not more than one million. The population of the countries they ruled must have been nearly two hundred million. Even if all the Mongol soldiers had been spread through the conquered countries they could still hardly have held them, even with the help of the Turkish nomads. But most Mongols returned after the campaigns to Mongolia. Historians used to write that the Mongol invasions happened because Central Asia became drier and less able to feed its population, but this is not true; the Mongols did not leave Mongolia to settle — only to raid and loot.

It was also too big in area. The Mongols set up a very elaborate postal service; everywhere there were stations with horses. Messengers travelled at great speed with information and orders. (D18) But, like other

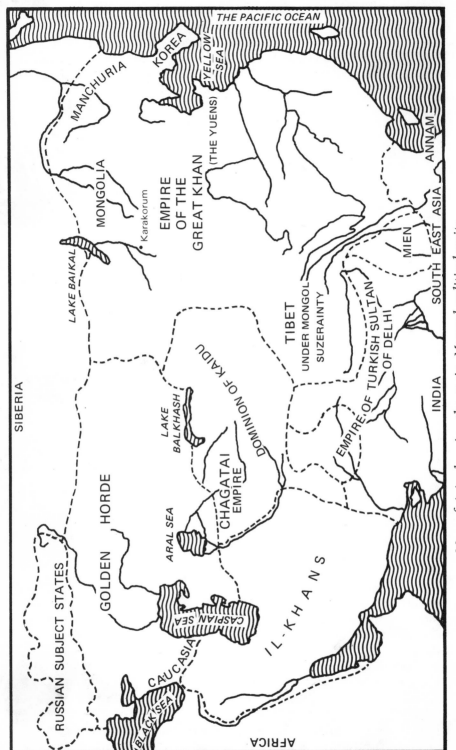

Map of Asia showing the main Mongol political units

THE PACIFIC OCEAN

SIBERIA

MANCHURIA

KOREA

YELLOW SEA

MONGOLIA

• Karakorum

LAKE BAIKAL

EMPIRE OF THE GREAT KHAN

(THE YUENS)

ANNAM

SOUTH EAST ASIA

MIEN

TIBET

UNDER MONGOL SUZERAINTY

DOMINION OF KAIDU

LAKE BALKHASH

CHAGATAI EMPIRE

ARAL SEA

EMPIRE OF TURKISH SULTAN OF DELHI

INDIA

RUSSIAN SUBJECT STATES

GOLDEN HORDE

IL-KHANS

CASPIAN SEA

CAUCASIA

BLACK SEA

AFRICA

The Tower of Skulls

empires before the invention of railways, aeroplanes and tele-phones, the problem of communi-cations remained.

At the best of times the Mongols could never really govern their empire. They just collected whatever taxes they could and spent the money on war, buildings and communications. In the end they could hardly find out what was happening before it was too late.

This shows us the importance of science and technology. It also explains why the Mongol empire was the last great nomad empire. From the fifteenth century fire-arms became steadily more im-portant in warfare; with that

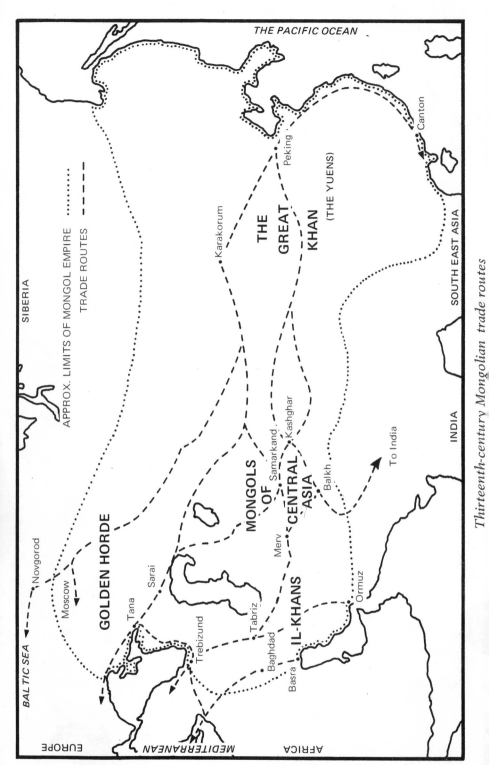

THE PACIFIC OCEAN

APPROX. LIMITS OF MONGOL EMPIRE ···········
TRADE ROUTES -------

SIBERIA

Canton

Peking

THE
GREAT
KHAN

(THE YUENS)

Karakorum

SOUTH EAST ASIA

INDIA

Samarkand
Kashghar

MONGOLS
OF
CENTRAL
ASIA

Balkh

To India

Merv

GOLDEN HORDE

Novgorod

Moscow

Sarai

Tana

Tabriz

IL-KHANS

Trebizund

Ormuz

BALTIC SEA

Baghdad

Basra

EUROPE

MEDITERRANEAN

AFRICA

Thirteenth-century Mongolian trade routes

change the nomad military superiority disappeared; research and factories were essential to develop firearms. People had to set aside some of their wealth to enable others to do the necessary work. Only settled people could do this adequately. In the end they would win.

THE MONGOL ACHIEVEMENTS

What did the Mongols do? First of all they destroyed other governments and put their own governments in their places. In China this was not the first time this had happened and after the Mongols were driven out China resumed her own ways under the Ming dynasty. In Russia there was a much greater change. Tatar rule destroyed the old trading states and to fight them the Russians had to organize themselves under the harsh rule of one city — Moscow — and the course of Russian history was altered.

Head of Tamurlane

Western Europe, which escaped the Tatar attacks, developed very differently. For the muslim world the Tatar invasions seemed like the end of the world and great changes followed. In Turkestan the effects were greatest of all. In the fourteenth century there came from Turkestan a new great conqueror — Timur or Tamerlane. There the nomads were dominant until the nineteenth century.

But the results were not only destructive. Before the Mongol conquests east and west had lived in ignorance of each other. The Mongols built something like a bridge across Asia. Italian merchants visited China and brought back news of its great civilization. (D19) Chinese inventions like printing, paper money, gunpowder and playing cards found their way to Europe. So unfortunately did the great plague of the Black Death in 1348. But, for a time, the Mongols made the world a smaller place.

Sextant in the Famous Observatory of Ulugbeg, Grandson of Timur

DOCUMENT 1

MONGOL APPEARANCE   *PREJEVALSKY – A nineteenth-century Russian soldier who travelled in Mongolia*

A broad flat face, with high cheek-bones, wide nostrils, small narrow eyes, large prominent ears, coarse black hair, scanty whiskers and beard, a dark sunburnt complexion, and, lastly, a stout thickset figure, rather above average height: such are the distinguishing features of this race.

The first thing which strikes the traveller in the life of the Mongol is his excessive dirtiness: he never washes his body, and very seldom his face and hands. Owing to constant dirt, his clothing swarms with parasites, which he amuses himself by killing in the most unceremonious way. It is a common sight to see a Mongol open his sheepskin or kaftan to catch an offending insect and execute him on the spot between his front teeth. The uncleanliness and dirt amidst which they live is partly attributable to their dislike, almost amounting to dread, of water or damp.

DOCUMENT 2

TENTS   *M. HUC – A nineteenth-century French missionary who travelled in Tibet and Mongolia*

The universal habitation of the Mongol is the felt tent or yurta, which is one shape throughout the country. It is round, with a convex roof, through an opening in which smoke escapes and light is admitted. The sides are of wooden laths, fastened together in such a way that, when extended, they resemble a lattice with meshes a foot square. This frame-work is in several lengths, which, when the yurta is pitched, are secured with rope, leaving room on one side for a wooden door three feet high, and about the same in width. The size of these dwellings varies, but the usual dimensions are from twelve to fifteen in diameter, and about ten feet high in the centre. The roof is formed of light poles attached to the sides and doorways by loops, the other ends being stuck into a hoop, which answers the double purpose of chimney and window.

When all is made fast, sheets of felt, of double thickness in winter, are drawn over the sides and door and round the chimney, and the habitation is ready. The hearth stands in the centre of the interior; facing the entrance are ranged the burkhans [gods], and on either side are the various domestic utensils. Round the hearth, where a fire is kept burning all day, felt is laid down; and in the yurtas of the wealthier classes even carpets for sitting and sleeping on. In these, too, the walls are lined with cotton or silk, and the floors are of wood.

This habitation is indispensable to the wild life of the nomad; it is quickly taken to pieces and removed from place to place, whilst it is an effectual protection against cold and bad weather. In the severest frost the temperature round the hearth is comfortable. At night the fire is put out, the felt covering drawn over the chimney, and even then, although not warm, the felt yurta is far more snug than an ordinary tent. In summer the felt is a good non-conductor of heat, and proof against heaviest rain.

The odour pervading the interior of the Mongol tents is, to those not accustomed to it, disgusting and almost insupportable. This smell, so potent sometimes that it seems to make one's heart rise to one's throat, is occasioned by the mutton grease and butter with which everything on or about a Tatar is impregnated. It is on account of this habitual filth, that they are called Stinking Tatars by the Chinese.

DOCUMENT 3

MONGOL CARTS   *WILLIAM OF RUBRUCK — A thirteenth-century Franciscan monk who travelled in the Mongol Empire*

And so on the third day after leaving Soldaia we came across the Tatars; when I came among them it seemed indeed to me as if I were stepping into some other world, the life and customs which I will describe for you as well as I can.

The Tatars have no abiding city nor do they know of the one that is to come. They have divided among themselves Scythia, which stretches from the Danube as far as the rising of the sun. Each captain, according to whether he has more or fewer men under him, knows the limits of his pasturage and where to feed his flocks in winter, summer, spring and autumn, for in winter they come down to the warmer districts in the south, in summer they go up to the cooler ones in the north. They drive their cattle to graze on the pasture lands without water in winter when there is snow there, for the snow provides them with water.

The dwelling in which they sleep has as its base a circle of interlaced sticks, and it is made of the same material; these sticks converge into a little circle at the top and from this a neck juts up like a chimney; they cover it with white felt and quite often they also coat the felt with lime or with white clay and powdered bone to make it a more gleaming white, and sometimes they make it black. The felt round the neck at the top they decorate with lovely and varied paintings. Before the doorway they also hang felt worked in multicoloured designs; they sew coloured felt on to the other, making vines and trees, birds and animals. They make these houses so large that sometimes they are thirty feet across; for I myself once measured the width between the wheel tracks of a cart, and it was twenty feet, and when the house was on the cart it stuck out at least five feet beyond the wheels on each side. I have counted to one cart twenty-two oxen drawing one house, eleven in a row across the width of the cart, and the other eleven in front of them. The axle of the cart was as big as the mast of a ship, and a man stood at the door of the house on the cart, driving the oxen.

DOCUMENT 4

MONGOL LIFE   *PREJEVALSKY*

Their only occupation and source of wealth is cattle-breeding, and their riches are counted by the number of their livestock, sheep, horses, camels, oxen, and a few goats. As all the requirements of life — milk and meat for food, skins for clothing, wool for felt, and ropes — are supplied by his cattle, which also earn him large sums by their sale, or by the transport of merchandise, so the nomad lives entirely for them. His personal wants, and those of his family, are of secondary consideration. His movements from place to place depend on the wants of his animals. If they are well supplied with food and water, the Mongol is content. His skill and patience in managing them are admirable. He loves and cherishes his animals; nothing will induce him to saddle a camel or a horse under a certain age; no money will buy his lambs or calves, which he considers it wrong to kill before they are full-grown.

The wildest steppe-horse cannot unseat its Mongol rider. He is in his element on horseback, going at full speed. He loves and understands horses; a fast galloper or a good ambler is his greatest delight, and he will not part with such a treasure, even in his direst need.

DOCUMENT 5

MONGOL WOMEN   *M. HUC*

Among the Tatars, household and family cares rest entirely upon the woman; it is she who milks the cows, and prepares the butter, cheese, etc.; who goes, no matter how far, to draw water; who collects the fuel, dries it, and piles it around the tent. The making of clothes, the tanning of skins, the fulling of cloth, all appertain to her; the sole assistance she obtains, in these various labours, being that of her sons, and then only while they are quite young.

DOCUMENT 6

MONGOL FOOD   *PREJEVALSKY*

Tea and milk constitute the chief food of the Mongols all the year round, but they are equally fond of mutton. The highest praise they can bestow on any food is to say that it is 'as good as mutton'. The favourite part is the tail which is pure fat. They have a remarkable way of killing their sheep; they slit up the creature's stomach, thrust their hand in, and seize hold of the heart, squeezing it till the animal dies. No part of the slaughtered animal is wasted, but everything is eaten up with utmost relish.

The gluttony of this people exceeds all description. A Mongol will eat more than ten pounds of meat at one sitting, but some have been known to devour an average-sized sheep in the course of twenty-four hours!

They always boil their mutton, only roasting the breast as a delicacy. On a winter's journey, when the frozen meat requires extra time for cooking, they eat it raw, slicing off pieces from the surface, and returning it again to the pot. When travelling and pressed for time, they take a piece of mutton and place it on the back of the camel, underneath the saddle, to preserve it from the frost, whence it is brought out during the journey and eaten, covered with camel's hair and reeking with sweat; but this is no test of a Mongol's appetite.

They eat with their fingers, which are always disgustingly dirty; raising a large piece of meat and seizing it in their teeth, they cut off with a knife, close to the mouth, the portion remaining in the hand.

On special occasions they eat the flesh of goats and horses; beef rarely, and camels' flesh more rarely still.

DOCUMENT 7

KUMISS   *WILLIAM OF RUBRUCK*

When they have collected a great quantity of milk, which is as sweet as cow's milk when it is fresh, they pour it into a large skin or bag and they begin churning it with a specially made stick which is as big as a man's head at its lower end, and hollowed out; and when they beat it quickly it begins to bubble like new wine and to turn sour and ferment, and they churn it until they can extract butter. Then they taste it and when it is fairly pungent they drink it. As long as one is drinking, it bites the tongue like vinegar; when one stops, it leaves on the tongue the taste of milk of almonds and greatly delights the inner man; it even intoxicates those who have not a very good head. It greatly provokes urine.

DOCUMENT 8

CHINGIS AND THE TATARS   *SECRET HISTORY — Written in 1240, an account of the years in which Chingis Khan became supreme*

Afterwards in the autumn of the Dog year [1201] Chingis faced in battle the White Tatars and three other Tatar tribes. Before the battle he gave these orders to his troops: 'If we are victorious, there must be no private looting. There will be an equal distribution of the booty when the campaign is over.'

They did defeat the Tatars, and completely pillaged the home-camps of the four Tatar tribes.

When he had pillaged the four Tatar tribes, Temujin [Chingis] held a secret council with his kinsmen and proposed as follows: 'As revenge for the slaying of our father by the Tatars it is now proper that we should put to death all their males who stand as high as the linch-pin of a cart. The rest, male and female, are to be used as slaves.'

DOCUMENT 9

CHINGIS BECOMES KHAN OF THE MONGOLS *SECRET HISTORY*

Altan, Khuchar, Sach-beki and all of them, after consulting together, said to Temujin, 'We appoint you as our Khan. If you will be our Khan, we will go as vanguard against the multitude of your enemies. All the beautiful girls and married women that we capture and all the fine horses, we will give to you. When hunting is afoot, we will be the first to go to the battle and will give you the wild beasts that we surround and catch. If in time of battle we disobey your orders or in time of peace we act contrary to your interests, part us from our wives and possessions and cast us out into the wilderness.' Such was the oath they made to serve him. They made him Great Khan, with the name of Chingis.

DOCUMENT 10

MONGOL WARFARE *WILLIAM OF RUBRUCK*

Chingis Khan ordained that the army should be organized in such a way that over ten men should be set one man and he is what we call a captain of ten; over ten of these should be placed one, named a captain of a hundred; at the head of ten captains of a hundred is placed a captain of a thousand, and over ten captains of a thousand is one man, and the word they used for this number means 'darkness'. Two or three chiefs are in command of the whole army, yet in such a way that one holds the supreme command.

When they are in battle, if one or two or three or even more out of a group of ten run away, all are put to death; and if a whole group of ten flees, the rest of the group of a hundred are all put to death, if they do not flee too. In a word, unless they retreat in a body, all who take flight are put to death.

They all have to possess the following arms at least: two or three bows, or at least one good one, three large quivers full of arrows, an axe and ropes for hauling engines of war. As for the wealthy, they have swords pointed at the end but sharp only on one side and somewhat curved, and they have a horse with armour; their legs also are covered and they have helmets and cuirasses. Some have cuirasses, and protection for their horses, fashioned out of leather.

Some of them have lances which have a hook in the iron neck, and with this, if they can, they will drag a man from his saddle. The length of their arrows is two feet, one palm and two digits. Since feet are not all the same, we will give the measurements of a geometrical foot: the length of a digit is two grains of barley, and sixteen digits make a geometrical foot. The heads of the arrows are very sharp and cut on both sides like a two-edged sword — the Tatars always carry files at the side of their quiver for sharpening their arrows. The iron heads have a pointed tail, a digit's breadth in length and this they stick into the shaft.

When they are going to make war, they send ahead an advance guard and these carry nothing with them but their tents, horses and arms. They seize no plunder, burn no houses and slaughter no animals; they only wound and kill men or, if they can do nothing else, put them to flight. They much prefer, however, to kill than to put to flight. The army follows after them, taking everything they come across, and they take prisoner or kill any inhabitants who are to be found. Not content with this, the chiefs of the army next send plunderers in all directions to find men and animals, and they are most ingenious at searching them out.

It should be known that when they come in sight of the enemy they attack at once, each one shooting three or four arrows at their adversaries; if they see that they are not going to be able to defeat them, they retire, going back to their own line. They do this as a blind to make the enemy follow them as far as the places where they have prepared ambushes. If the enemy pursues them to these ambushes, they surround and wound and kill them. Similarly if they see that they are opposed by a large army, they sometimes turn aside and, putting a day's or two days' journey between them, they attack and pillage another part of the country and they kill men and destroy and lay waste the land. If they perceive that they cannot even do this, then they retreat for some ten or twelve days and stay in a safe place until the army of the enemy has disbanded, whereupon they come secretly and ravage the whole land. They are indeed the most cunning in war, for they have now been fighting against other nations for forty years and more.

When, however, they are going to join battle, they draw up all the battle lines, just as they are to fight. The chiefs or princes of the army do not take part in the fighting but take up their stand some distance away facing the enemy, and they have besides them their children on horseback and their womenfolk and horses; and sometimes they make figures of men and set them on horses. They do this to give the impression that a great crowd of fighting men is assembled there. They send a detachment of captives and men of other nationalities who are fighting with them to meet the enemy head-on, and some Tatars may perhaps accompany them. Other columns of stronger men they dispatch far off to the right and the left so that they are not seen by the enemy and in this way they surround them and close in and so the fighting begins from all sides. Sometimes when they are few in number they are thought by the enemy, who are surrounded, to be many, especially when the latter catch sight of the children, women, horses and dummy figures described above, which are with the chief or prince of the army and which they think are combatants; and alarmed by this they are thrown into disorder. If it happens that the enemy fight well, the Tatars make a way of escape for them; then as soon as they begin to take flight and are separated from each other they fall upon them and more are slaughtered in flight than could be killed in battle. However, it should be known that, if they can avoid it, the Tatars do not like to fight hand to hand but they wound and kill men and horses with their arrows; they only come to close quarters when men and horses have been weakened by arrows.

All those they take prisoner in battle they put to death unless they happen to want to keep some as slaves. They divide those who are to be killed among the captains of a hundred to be executed by them with a battle-axe; they in their turn divide them among the captives, giving each a slave to kill ten or more or less as the officers think fit.

DOCUMENT 11

CHINGIS KHAN IN TURKESTAN *TABAKAT-I NASIRI – A thirteenth-century Muslim history written by Juzjani*

Trustworthy persons have related that Chingis Khan, at the time when he came into Khurasan, was sixty-five years old, a man of tall stature, of vigorous build, robust in body, the hair on his face scanty and turned white, with cats' eyes, possessed of great energy, discernment, genius, and understanding, awe-striking, a butcher, just, resolute, an overthrower of enemies, intrepid, sanguinary, and cruel. The Chingis Khan moreover in [the administration of] justice was such, that, throughout his whole camp, it was impossible for any person to take up a fallen whip from the ground except he were the owner of it; and, throughout his whole army, no-one could give indication of [the existence of] lying and theft.

DOCUMENT 12

CHINGIS KHAN IN TURKESTAN *TABAKAT-I NASIRI*

One day, during conversation [Chingis Khan] said to me: 'A mighty name will remain behind me in the world through taking vengeance upon Mohammad, the Robber [i.e., Sultan Muhammad, Khwarazm Shah]. The Khwarazm Shah was not a monarch: he was a robber. Had he been a monarch he would not have slain my envoys and traders who had come to Utrar for kings should not slay ambassadors.' I said: 'A name continues to endure where there are people, but how will a name endure when the Khan's servants martyr all the people and massacre them, for who will remain to tell the tale?

DOCUMENT 13

THE MONGOL ATTACK ON ISLAM   *IBN AL-ATHIR – A*
thirteenth-century Arab historian

It is unlikely that mankind will see the like of this calamity, until the world comes to an end and perishes. For even Antichrist will spare such as follow him, though he destroy those who oppose him; but these [Tatars] spared none, slaying women and children, ripping open pregnant women and killing unborn babes. For these were a people who emerged from the confines of China, and attacked the cities of Turkestan, like Kashghar and Balasaghun, and thence advanced on the cities of Transoxiana, such as Samarqand, Bukhara and the like; and of them one division then passed on into Khurasan, until they had made an end of taking possession, and destroying, and slaying and plundering, and thence passing on to Ray [Tehran], Hamadan and the Highlands, and the cities contained therein, even to the limits of Iraq whence they marched on the towns of Azherbayjan, destroying them and slaying most of their inhabitants, of whom none escaped save a small remnant; and all this in less than a year. And when they had finished with Azherbayjan they passed on to Derbend and occupied its cities, none of which escaped save the fortress wherein was their King; wherefore they passed by it to the countries of the Lan and the Lakiz and the various nationalities which dwell in that region [the Caucasus], and plundered, slew, and destroyed them to the full. And thence they made their way to the lands of the Qipchaq [the Ukraine], who are the most numerous of the Turks, and slew all such as withstood them, while the survivors fled to the fords and mountain-tops, and abandoned their country, which these Tatars overran. All this they did in the briefest space of time, remaining only for so long as their march required and no more.

Another division, distinct from that mentioned above, marched on Ghazna and its dependencies, and those parts of India, Sistan and Kirman which border thereon, and wrought therein deeds like unto the other, nay, yet more grievous. Now this is a thing the like of which ear hath not heard; for Alexander, concerning whom historians agree that he conquered the world, did not do so with such swiftness, but only in the space of about ten years; neither did he slay, but was satisfied that men should be subject to him. But these Tatars conquered most of the habitable globe, and the best, the most flourishing and most populous part thereof, and that whereof the inhabitants were the most advanced in character and conduct, in about a year; nor did any country escape their devastations which did not fearfully expect them and dread their arrival.

Stories have been related to me which the hearer can scarcely credit, as to the terror of them [*i.e,* the Mongols] which God Almighty cast into men's hearts; so that it is said that a single one of them would enter a village or a quarter wherein were many people, and would continue to slay them one after another, none daring to stretch forth his hand against this horseman. And I have heard that one of them took a man captive, but had not with him any weapon wherewith to kill him; and he said to his prisoner, 'Lay your head on the ground and do not move'; and he did so, and the Tatar went and fetched his sword and slew him therewith.

DOCUMENT 14

THE MONGOLS IN POLAND   *MATTHEW PARIS — A thirteenth-century monk and historian who lived at St Albans*

Frederick II, the Holy Roman Emperor, to Henry II of England [1241]

Their innumerable army is divided into three ill-omened portions, and, owing to the Lord's indulging them in their damnable plans, has proceeded thus divided. One of these has entered Poland, where the prince and duke of that country have fallen victims to their exterminating pursuers, and afterwards the whole of that country has been devasted by them. A second portion has entered Bohemian territory, where it is brought to a stand, having been attacked by the king of that country, who has bravely met it with all the forces at his command; and the third portion of it is over-running Hungary, adjoining to the Austrian territories. Hence fear and trembling have arisen amongst us, which calls upon us to arm. The certainty of the general ruin of the whole world, especially of Christendom, calls for hasty assistance and succour; for this race of people is wild, outlawed, and ignorant of the laws of humanity.

DOCUMENT 15

THE BATTLE OF LIEGNITZ   *MISCHOW: DE SARMATIA — A medieval Latin chronicle*

The two armies met on the broad plain of Gutfeld [Leichenfeld] on Monday, 9th April. Right at the beginning in the first encounter, the miners of Goldberg and others who did not possess armour were subjected to a shower of arrows from the Tatars, which left them lying like a cornfield struck by a hailstorm. Whereupon the two divisions led by Gulislav and the Duke of Oppela, Mieczyslav, attacked three of the Tatar divisions and inflicted on them such a beating that they turned in flight. But then a man (it is uncertain whether he was a Ruthenian, Russian or Tatar) rode at top speed in and out of the two divisions, screaming in a fearful voice, 'Flee! Flee!' and filled the Poles with terror. When Mieczyslav of Oppela heard this call he fled from the battle, taking a large number of his troops with him. When Duke Henry saw this he sighed and said 'It is all up with us'. He charged immediately with the remaining sound forces against the three Tatar divisions who had been engaged by the Polish divisions, and put them to flight. But the fourth Tatar division which was much larger than the others attacked under the leadership of Baidar with terrible violence and a hot, long-drawn-out struggle ensued. Then when a large part of the Tatars had fallen or had fled, there appeared a standard bearer, himself a giant in appearance, who waved a banner on which were Greek letters, and on top was fastened a model of a terrible black figure, with a long beard. Some magical device made the head of the figure shake about and from it there was emitted, suddenly, smoke and vapour with a horrible, unbearable smell, which poured over the Poles, rendering them helpless and incapable of continuing the struggle. Whereupon the Tatar army turned again upon the Poles with fearsome cries, broke through their ranks and wrought fearful slaughter among them, in the course of which Boleslav and many other knights were slain. Duke Henry himself was transfixed with a lance under the shoulder and fell dying from his horse. The Tatars lifted their raucous voices in an awful cry, dragged the Duke some little way from the battlefield, cut off his head with a sword, stripped the body of clothing and left the trunk to lie naked. . . . While they were collecting the booty, the Tatars, who had won so great a victory over the Poles, cut an ear off each of the corpses in order to count the number of the slain, and filled nine large sacks with them.

DOCUMENT 16

GUYUK KHAN TO POPE INNOCENT IV (1246)

WILLIAM OF RUBRUCK

Thou, who art the great Pope, together with all the Princes, come in person to serve us. At that time I shall make known all the commands of the Yasa.

You have also said that supplication and prayer have been offered by you, that I might find a good entry into baptism. This prayer of thine I have not understood. Other words which thou has sent me: 'I am surprised that thou hast seized all the lands of the Magyar and the Christians. Tell us what their fault is.' These words of thine I have also not understood. The eternal God has slain and annihilated these lands and peoples, because they have neither adhered to Chingis Khan, nor to the Great Khan [Ogetei], both of whom have been sent to make known God's command, nor to the command of God. Like their words, they also were impudent, they were proud and they slew our messenger-emissaries. How could anybody seize and kill by his own power contrary to the command of God?

Though thou likewise sayest that I should become a trembling Nestorian Christian, worship God and be an ascetic, how knowest thou whom God absolves, in truth to whom He shows mercy? How does thou know that such words as thou speakest are with God's sanction? From the rising of the sun to its setting, all the lands have been made subject to me. Who could do this contrary to the command of God?

Now you should say with a sincere heart: 'I will submit and serve you.' Thou thyself, at the head of all the Princes, come at once to serve and wait upon us! At that time I shall recognize your submission.

If you do not observe God's command, and if you ignore my command, I shall know you as my enemy. Likewise I shall make you understand. If you do otherwise, God knows what I know.

Seal

We, by the power of the eternal Tengri, universal Khan of the great Mongol Ulus — our command. If this reaches peoples who have made their submission, let them respect and stand in awe of it.

DOCUMENT 17

A RAID BY THE CRIMEAN TATARS IN 1769   *BARON DE TOTT*

An eighteenth-century French diplomat and soldier who accompanied the Tatars on their last great raid

We arrived at New Serbia, where the raid would bring injury on the unfortunate inhabitants, and a council of war was summoned to allocate the troops for the expedition. . . . It was decided that the irregular forces should cross the river, divide into many small units and cover the entire area of New Serbia, so as to burn the villages, and all the stored-up harvest, carry off the inhabitants and the herds. It was further decided that each soldier employed on the raid should have two associates with the rest of the army. By this arrangement everyone would get a share of the loot without any argument about its division.

It was fascinating to see the care, the patience and the extreme agility with which the Tatars sought to retain what they had captured. A single man was not inconvenienced by his capture of five or six slaves of all ages, sixty sheep and twenty cattle. The children's heads protruded from a sack tied to the pommel of the saddle, a young girl was seated in front held by the left arm, the mother on the crupper, the father on one of the lead horses, the son on another, sheep, cattle in front and nothing escaped under the vigilant eye of the shepherd of the flock.

DOCUMENT 18

MONGOL COMMUNICATIONS *MARCO POLO — A fourteenth-century Italian merchant and traveller*

From the city of Peking there are many roads leading to the different provinces, and upon each of these, that is to say, upon every great high road, at the distance of twenty-five or thirty miles, there are stations, with houses of accommodation for travellers, called yamb or post-houses. These are large and handsome buildings. At each station four hundred good horses are kept in constant readiness, in order that all messengers going and coming upon the business of the grand khan, and all ambassadors, may have relays, and, leaving their jaded horses, be supplied with fresh ones. Even in mountainous districts, remote from the great roads, where there are no villages, and the towns are far distant from each other, his majesty has equally caused buildings of the same kind to be erected, furnished with everything necessary, and provided with the usual establishment of horses. He sends people to dwell upon the spot, in order to cultivate the land, and attend to the service of the post; by which means large villages are formed. In consequence of these regulations, ambassadors to the court, and the royal messengers, go and return through every province and kingdom of the empire with the greatest facility and convenience, in all which the grand khan exhibits a superiority over every other emperor, king or human being. In his dominions no fewer than two hundred thousand horses are thus employed in the department of the post, and ten thousand buildings, with suitable furniture, are kept up. It is indeed so wonderful a system, and so effective in its operation, as it is scarcely possible to describe.

When it is necessary that the messengers should proceed with extraordinary dispatch, as in the cases of giving information of disturbances in any part of the country, the rebellion of a chief, or other important matter, they ride two hundred or sometimes two hundred and fifty miles in the course of a day.

THE JOURNEY FROM THE CRIMEA TO CHINA   *PEGOLOTTI –*
A fourteenth-century Italian merchant, who wrote a handbook for merchants

In the first place, you must let your beard grow long and not shave. And at Tana you should furnish yourself with an interpreter.

And from Tana travelling to Gittarchan you should take with you twenty-five days' provisions, that is to say, flour and salt fish, for as to meat you will find enough of it at all the places along the road. And so also at all the chief stations noted in going from one country to another in the route, according to the number of days set down above, you should furnish yourself with flour and salt fish; other things you will find in sufficiency, and especially meat.

The road you travel from Tana to Cathay is perfectly safe, whether by day or by night, according to what the merchants say who have used it.

ACKNOWLEDGMENTS

Illustrations

C.R. Bawden page 2; Thames and Hudson Ltd page 8 (both pictures)

Documents

George Allen & Unwin Ltd, *The Secret History of the Mongols* trans. Arthur Waley; Sheed & Ward, *The Mongol Mission* ed. Christopher Dawson

Greenhaven World History Program

History Makers
Alexander
Constantine
Leonardo Da Vinci
Columbus
Luther, Erasmus and Loyola
Napoleon
Bolivar
Adam Smith, Malthus and Marx
Darwin
Bismark
Henry Ford
Roosevelt
Stalin
Mao Tse-Tung
Gandhi
Nyerere and Nkrumah

Great Civilizations
The Ancient Near East
Ancient Greece
Pax Romana
The Middle Ages
Spices and Civilization
Chingis Khan and the Mongol Empire
Akbar and the Mughal Empire
Traditional China
Ancient America
Traditional Africa
Asoka and Indian Civilization
Mohammad and the Arab Empire
Ibin Sina and the Muslim World
Suleyman and the Ottoman Empire

Great Revolutions
The Neolithic Revolution
The Agricultural Revolution
The Scientific Revolution
The Industrial Revolution
The Communications Revolution
The American Revolution
The French Revolution
The Mexican Revolution
The Russian Revolution
The Chinese Revolution

Enduring Issues
Cities
Population
Health and Wealth
A World Economy
Law
Religion
Language
Education
The Family

Political and Social Movements
The Slave Trade
The Enlightenment
Imperialism
Nationalism
The British Raj and Indian Nationalism
The Growth of the State
The Suez Canal
The American Frontier
Japan's Modernization
Hitler's Reich
The Two World Wars
The Atom Bomb
The Cold War
The Wealth of Japan
Hollywood